Imaginary Paintings and Other Poems

For Aimee,

with much admiration
for your powerful and
heartfelt poems,

in friendship,

Charlie

April 6, 1990

Earlier versions of these poems have appeared in the following journals or publications:

ANTIOCH REVIEW: "Imaginary Painting: *Harvest Home.*"
THE BELOIT POETRY JOURNAL: "Falling Asleep in Michigan."
CALIBAN: "The Passionate Shopping Mall," "Translation from an Unknown Language: *The Man Who Sold His Bed.*"
CAROLINA QUARTERLY: "Imaginary Paintings: *Jesus and the Stone, Fleetwood Café,* and *Boredom of Dogs.*"
THE CHOWDER REVIEW: "New Age Poem" (published as "Narcissus as Hero").
COLUMBIA: "Unused Words"
DENVER QUARTERLY: "How She Knew It Was Over."
GULF COAST: "The Last String Quartet of Arnold Schoenberg"
THE IOWA REVIEW: "Imaginary Paintings: *Dr. Thomas Garvin and his Wife,* and *Black Canvas.*"
KAYAK: "Exasperated Political Poem" (published as "Against the President") and "Meditation on Pornography."
LITTLE CAESAR: "Search."
MICHIGAN BROADSIDES: (published by OtherWind Press, Inc.): "Color Slides of the Warm Climates."
THE MINNESOTA REVIEW: "Imaginary Painting: *Beggar in the Snow.*"
NORTHERN LIT QUARTERLY: "Coming Back to the Simple Things."
NORTHWEST REVIEW: "The Amnesia Plague."
THE PARIS REVIEW: "The Fables," "Machines That Make Men Happy," "The Photographer," "The Slow Classroom."
PEQUOD: "Imaginary Paintings: *River Rouge* and *Construction in Black and White.*"
POETRY: "Midwestern Poetics."
POETRY NORTHWEST: "Blind Boy Climbing a Watertower," "Fighting Depression, I Take My Family on a Picnic," "The Imaginary Friend," "Imaginary Painting: *The Convalescents.*"
SANTA MONICA REVIEW: "The Boy Who Didn't Drown"
SHENANDOAH: "Cantata at Midnight."

"How She Knew It Was Over," "The Slow Classroom," "The Fables," and "Color Slides of the Warm CLimates," have been reprinted in *The Third Coast II: Poetry by Michigan Writers,* published by The Wayne State Unviersity Press (Detroit: 1988).

Imaginary Paintings
and Other Poems

Charles Baxter

Paris Review Editions

Published by British American Publishing
3 Cornell Road
Latham, NY 12110
Manufactured in the United States of America

93 92 91 90 89 5 4 3 2 1

Library of Congress Cataloging-in-Publication Data

Baxter, Charles, 1947–
Imaginary paintings.

  I. Title.
PS3552.A854I53 1989   811'.54—dc   89-36127
ISBN 0-945167-24-5

for Al Greenberg
and
Bill Truesdale

Contents

IV Imaginary Paintings

V

I

Color Slides of the Warm Climates

The chipped black iron fence
around the mayor's house
throws down this spray of shadow
across the lawn, on which blue
and orange birds parade and feed.
The tiled roof is hammered silver.
Here is a plaque: such-and-such a date,
such-and-such a place, in ornamental
Spanish. Off to the right-hand side
a beggar sleeps. It's evening,
six o'clock, when charity
is at a minimum,

and here is the fountain del
Cielo, also with its beggars,
its scalloped and broken marble,
its fundamental light.
The water sprays
at noon and three o'clock
and all day Sunday.
The pumping station has been bombed
or is damaged or is merely
in a state of disrepair:
it is a hobby of the North American
to notice everything that doesn't

work. The air is fleshy pink
from bauxite dust
down at the harbor, where boy soldiers
nervously patrol imaginary lines,
whereas on the hotel terrace
the formal waiter smiles and smiles.
In shantytown at night, a lecture
motors through the streets,
a voice flowering from a truck.
It says history is the jacaranda's
root and trunk, the sorrow bird
singing in the mangrove swamp,

whose history is in the eye
atop the pyramid on the dollar bill.
This picture, light blue above,
cerulean below, is the posted beach
where no one swims
this time of year, and this
is the crucified black Jesus
painted in excited toy colors, and called
the blue Christ child
of the broken mountains. His foot
is smooth and almost disarticulated

from having been so often kissed.
Mesquite, a footpath, a dry arroyo.
Slogans painted
on the sewer pipe, sprayed on the mayor's
house: land and sun and ownership
and God the conqueror who comes
in a raised and gilded throne
lifted by the children he has cured.
Ecstasy and rapture
of the sun. "Hey, mister!"
This is a hand raised up for change:
photographed, and taken home.

Coming Back to the Simple Things

The scene would be midnight, early summer,
there in the kitchen under the yellow
light, two people standing in bathrobes
who are still lovers for now,
for this one hour in June,
with food placed on the table, two sandwiches
he might have made as a gift for her.

He will be talking. He will tug at his hands
as if the hands too have something to say,
the stutter of palms and of fingernails,
and he will want to say this:
something about time and forgetting
in words so uncertain it cannot matter.
He will lean forward at five
past midnight and ask, "When will we come back
to the simple things, when will it happen?"

But then it will be as if she hardly sees him,
as if he had been carried away, as if
she sits alone, an old woman rubbing
her fingers too small for their rings,
wrapped with tape so she won't lose them.
She tries to remember the question the man
in the bathrobe once asked her
but all she remembers are his hands
and their strange fretwork and kindling.
Then his words: "What are the simple things?
What are they? Where do we get them?"

The Passionate Shopping Mall

There was a scream and a cry
and the sound of shoes running on cleaned
marble, and there was a woman
with straight gray hair held back
with a braid wandering toward the fountain

where she washed her hands again and again,
and there was a child named Lonnie
who bought an airplane and whose mother beat him
in the aisle, and there was light
from nowhere that fell all over everything.

You could tell how serious the mall was
by the way people got lost there,
wondering where the light had come from
and what they had driven there to do,
and you could tell that the teenagers kissing

each other didn't exactly want to, but went on
because someone told them. Maybe it was
the shoes. Maybe people came to see
the clothes and the colors and felt bad
about themselves and decided not to have

affairs but to spend money instead. Maybe
the mall said, "People are ugly
fundamentally." Anyway, there's still
the little girl in pink pushing the plastic
seal on wheels, and an old woman who won't

stop mumbling and sixteen TV sets
tuned to the same channel. Maybe the mall
owns the colors and just won't sell them.
It is a world of pianos and barbells
and dust going home in bags in a fury.

Unused Words

1

Forbearance

A grandfather
loitering in his day-old wrinkled suit
at the abrupt and stony seashore visited
without hope in late cut-rate October,
and a child who clutches
at this quiet and vested man, this screaming
child who will grow up—unlike the rest—
to go on screaming. The gulls are circling,
but this man, our subject, utters not one word.
There is something patient and empty in the waves,
which his face imitates.
This child, screaming at the waves,
grows up to be someone's mad great uncle
who is appointed to a life of celestial terror
and it's in the rain that one feels the power
of forbearance, in this autumn drizzle
soaking this grave grandparent to the skin,
loving what is damaged and wholly his
and held like a broken pocketwatch
tightly in his hand.

2

Rectitude

If no one says it,
no one has it. It must have gone
to the granite rocks over which
the water pounds. Think of it as stone
and how our ancestors wanted to be stones.
They wished to be unbending: we see this
in the photographs in which they do not smile.
It's in the clothes, the stove-
pipe hats and veils and woolen scarves
and the remorseless lack of color they
favored to represent themselves—they were
stiff and hated color because the world
was black and white, the right side
and the wrong, and they told each other
so. By God there was the law.
Of course they were all a class
of worriers—the sky despite their arguments
is blue and does not always fall—
but still they had those eyes.
The eyes survive in photographs.
They say *stone* and *wind* and *pain.*
Even a scowl is a kind of style.

3

Sorrow

It's a week of Mondays, and all the slopes are pitched uphill,
and every night the dinner's burned,

and no one has a clue why it's November
all this year, accompanied by this epidemic

slush and mud, snow that falls through fog,
deer crippled on the lethal freeway

that careens to that factory city where I once held you.
There might be sun, but, yes, it's gone, and the dew

is freezing so that grasses scrape their blades
together, a sclerotic sound. A sparrow pecks

at birdbath ice, then calls: a frozen melody iced
in frozen air. Sister word of "weary,"

sorrow separates the lovers' flesh with snow
that falls and melts and falls again through fog

viewed from a frosted window by someone not quite there
not quite here, not quite now.

4

Mercy

Portia's word,
so stamped with her particular design
that gradually it faded from
common use into the law,
the theater of crimes. Only
governors have it now—
stays of execution passed on
the phone. But this morning
I see it as a hand that rises
into the air with the sun
in a fiery nimbus behind
the hand, and because I claim
nothing outside the text,
all things will live, not just
the fine. I will not let
the fingers make a fist. I write
these words, I claim them. If I say
the hand stays open, it is so.

The Photographer

"But when I concentrate on what
is now in my mind, what
instructions can be found there?"
      —Saul Kripke, *Wittgenstein on Rules and Private Language*

1.

He knows the tricks for lighting a child: he must aim
the reflector lamps so the face
shades back on both sides, is bright with its
interior grace, its announcement of being; he
aims light at the ceiling, at the floor, to avoid
what amateurs do: to light the child
from the front, like an oncoming car, like
the child's future speeding toward the photographer's
studio with its stinging flash already
out of the case, ready to burst
and wash out the comforting depth
and leave the face a white image on white paper.

2.

He knows French. He says to himself, "Les mystères
de peau," and sometimes, "Les mystères de chair."
The trick to posing newlyweds . . . but everyone
knows how you must incline them
to lean imperceptibly toward the warm flesh
of the other and how their smiles must
learn to be solemn: this is a bow

to the world's gravity, this is skin meeting skin
and saying, "I promise." He distrusts laughter
in newlyweds; he takes down their faces
and makes a prediction. "Those," he says, pointing
at four hands, two gleaming smiles. "A year and a half."

3.

This began with a woman. This started the summer
he at last lost himself in what he had always
imagined: *light knows nothing,* carries no thought,
is only the touch of a wave off a surface.
He posed her near the window's gardenias
with her hand lifted in what he believed
was a womanly gesture. He stood her nude near
the stairs, nude on the arm of the sofa. After
she left him, he learned to photograph children,
and now at home he says, *See,* as he shows you
a shot of a doorknob, of a dish, of a pencil,
a bowl in the half-dark. Look, he says,

simple objects, the world's wonders, can you believe it?

Blind Boy Climbing a Watertower

The day smells like a rusty iron leaf.
Wind vibrates the watertower
until it is a giant's doublebass
whose only note says, "Climb,"
a word sworn in secret to the boy,
not to his brothers, who are dull
because they work all day, because they see.

Barefoot, to feel the ladder's rungs
nestle warmly against his calloused heels,
he lifts himself, hand over spider hand,
above his father's unimaginary farm
where his brothers spread cow manure,
check their watches, wait for lunch,
and hand down clothes sleepily to him.

He has heard of clouds: like giants
they are imaginary and as remote
as spectral rainbows. He listens
for the cars that speed like sound
down the highway half a mile away.
The boy thinks about their girls.
He is sixteen and goes nowhere without a comb.

With his fingers to his face,
he feels handsome to himself. His brothers
say he's vain, and his father says
looks aren't worth thinking on.
Fearless of heights he's never seen,
he catapults himself onto the tiny walkway
circling the tank. He hears a colossal

breath blow underneath his feet
that implicates the sky, the atmosphere
and whatever must be blue. He waves
from his castle turret at the whine of cars,
at imaginary sunburnt girls
who would call like sirens to bring him down,
earth songs of light and sex and gravity.

The Lady with the Dog

She lives locked with her lover's body
held secretly inside her, his face and hands
that no one else notices
tucked under her skin.
In public you can see her shampooing the dog
in a copper tub on the lawn, or down
on her knees weeding the vegetable garden,
but he is the unnamed weight she carries
place to place as a dark passenger,

and he too walks on the street
with his lover sealed inside him
and her secret hands pressed outwards
so that every inch of her memorized skin
makes him absent and quiet.
These captured, dreamy strangers wander the streets
too deep in the wars of love to have an opinion,

but they both wake, far from each other,
in that eerie moment before dawn
when the birds fly suddenly upwards toward something silent,
as if they see the whole hopelessness of the day
pulling hard at the sun,
dragging it above the horizon
for the loveless business of work and forgetting.

Falling Asleep in Michigan

This time it's someone cradled into himself
on his bed, the homework breathing
like a bad pet he can't train
over there, on his desk.
                              This is in Flint
where outside the boy's window
                              the same car
can turn at a corner night after night

with its taillights tied on with clothesline,
and the boy, Laszlo, never knows
who the strange man with a scar is
                              behind the wheel,
and he doesn't know where he's going.
Instead of homework, he doodles:

he draws a girl alive in the trunk,
because otherwise life would be what
his mother has told him it is: hard,
                              always the same,
no surprises. Laszlo wants to doze off

and pry open the trunk and let her out
for the adventure, so he can slick back his hair and show
something
wild like an earring

and a black shirt with no buttons,
and a bed,
      and twilight,
            and his hands' cleverness,

so he can say, "Whatever weird
stuff comes up in this dream,
jesus, I'll take it,
      no kidding."

Midwestern Poetics

The unpromising meets the unexotic,
and we are home again, alone,
with this image of the possible:
these hills that anyone can climb,
the lowlands, reeds perched with red-wing
blackbirds, leading painlessly
to cemeteries and small towns
where voices are subdued and have no region.
A man paints enormous replicas
of Rembrandt's middle period on the sides
of barns. He is mad. He leaves.

Without elevations, hurricanes, or
earthquakes, without geological alarms,
we learn to count the angles
in the sky and to admire four-barrel carburetors
in the muscle cars that combine with roadside
trees in the six-pack dark of Saturday.
It's not that something has to happen.
A man writes a letter to himself
and excludes the absolute: he is four seasons,
paths in third-growth woods, nature
that is endlessly familiar.

He is a silo: he stores, he feeds.
No horsemen raging down the mountains
flying banners, no vipers, just this and that
that could be anywhere but happen to be here.
The children grow up calm: they learn
about psychotic tantrums like tornadoes.
They plan. There is time, and more time
and more time after that to learn to love
the mild gifts—these apple trees, these
sparrows—in this marriage with a woman
who knows you, but will not kiss you back.

The White Apartment

I'm like everybody. For example I passed that forest
without looking up—they rushed flickering past, those trees,
day after day like something merely in the way of the sun.
And when they were gone, from the cleaned, bottomed-out
land filled with pipes and a sign and cement,
I was like everyone, and I missed them,
and the scruffy brush and the snow that sat in there melting
and doing nothing and not developing.

Brick layered upon stone and mortar, and I watched it,
day after day on my way to work, my foot on the gas,
this construction, my windshield wipers
brushing away the rain that also fell
on the relentless workmen hammering in balconies
and bathrooms and digging one more hole for the pool.
At first it felt like a diversion. I wanted to say
it was wrong, but the radio was on

and there was music and soft advice about love and school.
Then one morning I pulled over and watched these kids
moving in (it was done by then, painted and scrubbed),
and I was like everyone, I saw them unloading
the truck and carrying her boxes of placemats
and his cartons of trophies into that uninhabited place
where nothing had ever been spilled or stained
and even the trees were new, to replace the old ones.

And on my way in I thought of how they were setting up shop
the way everyone does (but of course that's wrong, it's not
everyone, and that's part of the problem), but I saw
them touching each other in public, and maybe he stops
or she does, to stare at the not-quite-right sky
or to listen to the freeway noise (it's nearby; it's always
nearby) as familiar as an empty bucket of fried chicken
or the sound of Mahler from a battery radio.

And there's that newborn smell—I've smelled it—
almost a smile, of formaldehyde that bonds
particle board inside the new latex
gloss walls into which the woman (I was imagining
her now) in the ponytail hammers a nail so she can
hang immediately this photo
of someone she hardly remembers,
the past's ambassador, her grandmother,

who must certainly have loved her.
Who must also have loved the sound
of cicadas in August that thrill here
in small trees fresh from the nursery
that were dug and planted last week, or yesterday.
I was like that. I lived in the blank slate
near the paradise lawns between the truck and the door
and I watched the insects, those dying senators,

lie sideways in the suburban sun with one wing beating.
I was the age when you think that beneath the building
the ghosts of feed corn and those of soybeans
invert themselves and tease down steadily into rock . . .
spirit plants rooted in air and bearing fruit
in the stone, in the shale, that hard outer core of the world.
Above them, in the white apartment, no ghosts,
no memories, a casual nest

of a bed and dishes and one TV. I'm like anyone
who checks the walls that look back at him with all their blank
faces put on straight, and he thinks
That can't be right. He shakes his head and smiles.
She's unpacking plates and I'm halfway in to work,
trying to imagine them into happiness, and it's my fault,
because it's *not* my life, and after all
many people sit down with empty grins,

the guilty innocents. I want them gone, and the trees
returned, and so one last time I imagine them:
she smiles, lets down her hair, lets it fall on him,
and as he lies down with her the walls seem
like patient screens, unwritten books,
paychecks from God written illegibly in sun.
You've lived there. Yes, you, too.
Something was cleared away so you could thrive

in the room where you are sitting now, in that chair.
At twilight we come home to the one place
where we aren't tourists—where we say "home" and "love"
and we try to mean it. Here we are.
Listen: the dog star wind shivers
in the infant trees outside, dog-days,
late summer winds when someone comes home and kisses you.
The wind is here, invisible, then gone.

II

A Minor Character

1

"She could not help respecting the composure with which he
sat there, drinking his soup. If he wanted soup, he asked for
soup. Whether people laughed at him or were angry with him
he was the same."
                                        —Virginia Woolf, *To the Lighthouse*

        The stubborn falling of the snow:
a gradual accumulation on the grass
        until the green was covered

        and sidewalks disappeared below
the soft and silent drifting mass.
        Immobilized, and severed

        from the others in whose minds
the snow would never fall, he sat
        in secrecy, at dinner, as he endured

        the blizzard in his head, and winds
and drifts that covered houses, cats
        and cardinals and trees, covered

        everything, until the world
became a snowy desert, a plain of white,
        a crystalline horizon below

        which, awake and avalanched, men curled
up and waited. He ate politely and held the night-
        mare fondly before he let it go.

2

Dressed in vacation clothes for the disaster, and wearing smiles
for a sort of remnant party on the lawn,
they talk of war and politics, and weather, or the styles
of this year's music and cuisine. Only he is drawn—
the old man—down to the water to see the waves
falling, always falling, on some rock,
like the victims of the recent war, dead in trenches, cave-
like tunnels, or assembled and transported home in shock.
A stoic arranger of the adjectives, he hopes a phrase
for this world's losses will arrive, a poisoned butterfly
to catch and pin, but the light darkens and the water says,
"No, not now," to all that unhappiness tempered by
formality, and the struggle up Parnassus like an Alp—
a man for whom rhyme and rhythm are no help.

3

"Mr. Carmichael had 'lost all interest in life.' What did it
mean—that? she wondered . . . Had he turned pages over and
over, without reading them, sitting in his room in St. John's
Wood alone?"

—*To the Lighthouse*

In half dark the pages turn
    of their own free will,
a long history of Napoleon,
    and on the sill

a cigarette left burning.
    Napoleon: first born
then crowned before his exile
    and now gone.

Another life, a thousand pages
    saying so.
The pages turn. What do they really say?
    There's a glow

from the old man's cigarette,
    and, outside, a sound,
a cricket in the dawn or twilight.
    The daily bound-

ary to time is faded, lost. The insect
        and the emperor, almost
the same, viewed from this distance,
        although the cost

of one was greater: the usual cities
        burned, the jewels, crowns,
and deaths. Is it dawn or dusk?
        Again the sound

like charcoal of the cricket, and outside
        the humans pass.
Another book, another cigarette
        and the mass

of words marching single file
        from left to right.
All flesh is grass, the cricket sings,
        welcoming the night.

4

"He took opium."
                    —*To the Lighthouse*

Watching the ocean swell, then freeze
before the breakers come clamoring into shore,
he turns away; this takes hours; and the trees
toward which his gaze has wandered are also paralyzed.
Not a branch moves, not a sprig. There may be more
movement skyward, but the sun in its morning climb
is rimmed with frost at noon, or nine
and has stopped stock-still. Can this be analyzed

or simply dreamed? The land of dreams! What are its fountains,
wreathed and abstracted? Does the old man wake
to wakefulness or to another sleep, stained
with frozen words? In this cave the words are walls
of ice through which the winds, dull sobbing drafts, make
their way downward to stone pools, where they die.
He's still sleeping on the lawn; he opens up one eye,
and, still sleeping, walks down oak panelled halls

into the library. The books are shelved forever
and are infinitely high; there is no place the books are not;
they are every size. He wants to sleep inside a letter
or move himself bodily into a line by Coleridge or Blake.
He wakes again. Fifty feet away, one child has fought
another and is sobbing: well, apparently the sun *has* moved,
the breakers have resumed their work, and life is proved
to be, not a still life, but otherwise. He wants to take

the child in hand and comfort him with tales of crystal
domes and caves of ice, but the boy has instantly recovered
and is shouting and kicking at some ball.
Child work. The murdered trees come back to life; the breeze
returns; subterranean pastiche is smothered
by the grace of light and air, and the old man rises
from where he slept to hear the cacophonic cries
of gulls. For now he will see exactly what the others see.

5

Permanently post-war
and with no plans,
he comes back to the summer house this one last time
to gaze at the nonhuman:
sky and rock and sand—
the water washing in and taking things away—
tide pools reflecting a daytime moon.
He bows heavily and says hello
to the existing men and women who say the same to him.
The world's been burned,
yet it seems the war is never over
as long as everyone's inscripted
with the same old words,
"death" and "love" with the same bewildered gestures.
When will anyone be original again?
His orders are obscure:
no one below, no one above.
Formal and Edwardian,
and his despair
in such bad taste he will not mention it to anyone,
he sits quietly, not being a bother,
while the air and sky fall over him,
collapse, in a kind of tenderness,
and the sun does exactly what it's always done.
Nature will have its insurrection
years from now:
the sky will fall, and fall, and fall,

but he'll be gone.
For a moment all the dark-
ness drops away, and the specific
and exacting southwest wind lifts
his old outmoded antique soul
straight into blessedness: calm in the shifting breeze,
and blessings in the pure light and hopelessness of things.
He lifts his hand
toward this ordinary scene
of sky and water, people muddling about.
Without their knowing it, being polite,
he mutters words—who knows what?—
heading who knows where,
his prayer, not being sentimental,
asking nothing, knowing nothing,
but still pleased at least for being awake.
As the boat lands at the lighthouse
this minor character
stands and mutters names of colors
to the gods,
his heart holding the remaining world
suspended,—only for a moment
does it seem clear, this scene,
this afternoon, sixteen minutes past
three o'clock, 1919.

III

Meditation on Pornography

Beauty has been caught by the eye, and the eye,
attached to the head, has dragged the whole body along

to the source of beauty, the wide sheath of skin.
These heads might as well be joined at the mouth,
witness Paolo and Francesca, witness anyone,
tongues fastened thickly together in unapproachable dark.

Look! doves, summoned by desire, come with wings poised
and motionless to the sweet nest, borne by their will
through the air, while the hand sweeps
over the breast, and another hand inspects the curve of the
    shoulders.

In this act, this man and this woman feel their bodies
as a collection of parts. Head touches head,
hand reaches for hand, but nothing, ever, is joined.

Each one is wrapped in separate skin.
They feel their bodies' separateness, as we feel
our separation from them. So there must be
more porn, to suggest community somewhere,
a magical glue to provide visual bonds.
It must go on and on. It is hell

to be in the audience, not in the story,
it is hell to have a window to heaven and not to get in.
Who cares what they are really feeling in heaven?

They aren't feeling us. Maybe they only pretend.
But they don't feel like watching anything else
as the damned do, slumped in the FINE ARTS downtown.

The Man Who Couldn't Hold a Job

At ten o'clock he would always give up
and untie his apron and head home.
She'd be there
when he got back: he would raise
his slender pale hands in front
of her and ask, "What's the use?"
He wasn't tough although he could fix cars
and ring bells and cook hamburger, but only
for a few hours, until the day
suddenly became hard in its heat or cold
and he felt like a child who wants to explore
a forest that is not severe
where all the colored stones have names
and nobody stands up before being stupid.

When he was a boy, he'd sit
at the upstairs window facing the street
and ask, "Where are they all going?"
as the fathers and mothers drove past,
and now, with a son, he must watch
as the woman who will not agree
to be his wife brings out her breast,
smooth and swollen, to the baby's mouth.
When he walks outside, he doesn't believe
all those buildings the young men have made
with their hands and tools
are as beautiful as the men claim they are.
He thinks the men could have stayed home.

The Imaginary Friend

The imaginary friend at a piano.
Her fingers crouch on the keys in an awkward way.

Something about her face—
that bewildered look—

makes you think she lacks the training
to strike the notes she is sure she hears.

All her music is approximate.
The hands rest there, immobilized,

while outside a peculiar set of orange clouds
is passing, and a feeble-minded child plays with a stick.

The clouds and child contain a music,
but she can never get it down

the complicated arc of nerves
to that registry of keys.

Her body will not be the medium for what she feels.
The imaginary friend stays there

paralyzed, before the possibility of music,
the possibility of squeezing what is inside out.

The music of the poem is her abstracted look,
her persistence, what will be her heroism

in sitting there, tone deaf, playing tunes
that don't exist, unheard and beautiful.

Fighting Depression,
I Take My Family on a Picnic

There must be happiness. I will force happiness
into a package wrapped in waxed paper.
I will arrange water to cascade nearby
and to rush eagerly over stones and loose gravel.
Now if only the planets would huddle together
I know we would rise like feathers, like angels.

I will drive. Breakdowns everywhere on the highway,
and a radio report that something immense is missing.
My wife and son point—there!—to the table. We stop.
I spread out the red checkerboard cloth
and think of chess, how the innocent king
is mated by the equally innocent army, then trapped

on the board, and I pour my son his water
and explain the name of a bird. I keep myself secret.
I won't trouble them with this room upstairs
where the lonely buzzsaw touches tree after tree.
I put together his bread, fetch a bandaid,
and tell him that that plum won't ever be poison.

In Ravel, the waltzes tend to be frantic.
And remember those trolls in "Rip van Winkle"?
How they spent their time bowling, but couldn't smile?
Rip aged by sleeping. He learned to be stranger.
Now notice the loud softball and the storm about to explode,
but in this, as in every true picnic,

the storm passes away. I shoo a starved dog.
This place is heavily funny: even the leaves shake
and the vans grunt with mechanical cheer.
Is it cold on the rings of Saturn?
As cold as here? I wave at a bee,
at a wasp. Go away.

The strain of not weighing down others
with one's own weight! I promise to dip
in the river, the dirty green Huron, flowing somewhere
seeking a break in the ground,
a tunnel to earth's intimate, compressed core.
I make a face. They're all laughing at me.

I promise to buy a fudge-buster going home
but they doze, as we travel sunburned, carrying ants,
itchy, murmuring pledges at each other.
I will carry my son to his bed, I will
cheerfully take them all in,
I will not pull them out, here, to this sea.

County Road H

We are driving a gray road at night,
no signs, far from friends, out in the broken
country where trees whose names we don't know
ridge marshlands, shadow on shadow. Something
moves back and forth in the trees, ruffled
and winglike, which we might see
if we stopped. We don't. Sparrows fly up
in front of us—we know their names
and we name them—and though we are lost,
we are given the lights every half mile
of a window, a house, where someone may
still be watching for us, bent over a table,
cutting a fabric or reading the paper.
She lifts her head, listening
to the sound of a car that rises
in greeting and then starts falling away.
                                        Where
are we? you ask. We need to get home,
surfaces to polish, small stones
to break into tinier and heavier stones.
The road's scurf rises behind us,
and your face hints that at last
it may be all right to be lost, beyond everything.
But then you see: an animal stands
at the road's edge, her calm eyes unflinching,
her whole body resolved and unstartled.
I admit it: I drove here without a direction
having hoped for mild eyes to come out of the dark
and pass by us before we were gone.

The Slow Classroom

You could see windstorms and a piece of floating string
making their way to the school
for hours—you could watch the sun,
and the teacher agreed. She had
no ideas either. Everything that happened
took a week in that air, in that frame
of bulletin boards and tiny fluorescent lights,
but when you found a pencil at least
that's what you had, a pencil. They planned the day
for some hours but usually they just said, "Be here."

A plant grew quietly on the windowsill, and everybody
knew it was a good soldier and they nodded hello
if they were standing there and thought it was trying
hard. Where was Hawaii, or any worldly place?
They didn't bring maps. They had a story
about people and what they did, rushing around
in that terrible way they all have
on their business, but no one remembered it.
We were distracted: you could hear

the long arc of water shooting out
of the neighbor's sprinkler and saying, "Why not,"
and you could hear Johnny, my cousin,
who stood at the burnt low end of the playground
stupefied, counting leaves on one sumac after another,
while around him people were busy
making themselves into blurs. And one time they
brought God into the class but all he did
was look at us. And then he wandered away.

The Amnesia Plague

---

after García Márquez

Yes, already they are forgetting
you, and already your face fades
into dim clay. Already your mother
cannot quite picture your smile
or the line of your eyebrows, the cheek
she kissed after nursing reminds her
of the blankness of Asia, and your body
falls down a long cliff away
from where she can see it. Your hands
leave behind no electrical image,
and your father, when he breathes
the used-up oxygen of Friday,
thinks of a warm presence
where his lungs used to expand,
but you are gone, and he won't remember
that when you slept on his chest
you rose and fell on the seawaves
of breath. The old misplace
how you arrived and shouted
"I'm here!" and the young,
your brothers and wives,
open the door after you ring
and then they turn, shouting,
"Dear, there's someone outside."
If the earth holds you up
momentarily, it daydreams

with a low humming you cannot hear
of all the millions it has let fly
free of its history,
stories blown clear of the light,
anonymous as any bird or leaf.

At the Center of the Highway

Suppose the salesmen are the real explorers
at the eroded shore of absence

having known the center line of highways from birth
as blank as the hollowing at the heart of cells

it's why Americans always keep the radio on
and why money has a slightly irrelevant feel

we came to the country of absence and unfurled our flag
before putting the production line into motion on Sundays

because no one believes a drink helps at the day's end
and because warehouses at least have a purpose in life

say that it's hollow and they'll just laugh
as they do at embarrassing obvious sunsets

which is why if you tilt American heads backwards
American eyes, like dolls' eyes, snap shut suddenly

The Fables

They had princes in them, and talking ducks,
and there was always a jewel that someone had to kiss
at an angle. The king said, "Yes, here I am,"
and later, after the first bloody war was won,
he said, "We need more laws now. See to it."
The young man and the young woman
who met weeping in the dark snowy field
glanced up to watch an owl hooting at star-
light. They ran away, into the point at
the foot of the page. The fables ended when
the water in the stories flowed out of the rivers
back into the lakes, and stayed there.

And then I am closing my book in the room
I share with my brother, who is gluing a model plane
he will hang from the ceiling, and I look
at my hands, and I think of them as faithful
servants—hands and fingers. My brother
holds up the balsa wood fuselage to me,
and I nod, and there, in the electric light,
the world is not an example of anything. My
mother's voice calls us to dinner, and we both
stand, my brother and I, faithful now
to reality, to the chairs where we sit,
to the fables of what has already happened.

New Age Poem

In the war of form against content,
no one suffers. No bones are broken,

the bones are just taken away,
the arteries are taken away, and the war concludes

in laughter as the inside of everything
is carted off to the furnaces.

Now, in the aftermath, the world of surfaces
glimmers with an odd, ex-terrestrial vitality,

and with nothing to enter or to go into,
one becomes a film, a courageous coat of paint.

Though the domino principle tells of the death
of God and rugged individuals and the lowly subject,

there are still people dressed up
in outfits, as if they meant it,

who would give answers if they could talk.
But a pleasant Zen silence rules

except when Brueghel's dancers cross at the light,
making almost no sound in their jogging shoes.

The world of meaning is finally conquered
by just forgetting about it,

by not even bothering,
so that one must imagine even Narcissus

happy, as he stares into the water
and beats his breast,

because the water's surface spreads out his image,
and the waves break with his face.

The Purest Rage

This thing happens in mid-summer,
and at an intersection under a washed-out sky
lit as usual by the chafing sun,
and we're all lined up at one red light.
We're being dutiful, and it's July,
as if the gods told God it would have to be like this,
and then they died, and it still is.
I'm on my way to fill the lawn mower's can
with antique, lethal, leaded gasoline.

All these cars have their drivers' windows down,
and it's a battle of the bands; Van
Halen over here, and (I think) Sting,
cacophony pleasing to the ear, but then
I notice on my left this Riviera, a living room
on wheels, windows closed to keep the cool air in.
I look over: *he* and *she,*
both oddly young, and she, not driving,
is shouting patiently, her eyes fixed straight ahead.
I read her lips. The only word I see is "Yes."

Still the background of the music,
and her silent shouting whose pure rage
makes her neck cords stand out visibly and tight,
and I think, *she's my age.* I glance
at the man behind the wheel, absorbing this,
glasses, slicked hair, white shirt, blue silk tie.
And then they're gone, and I'm being honked at,
and I accelerate, wanting to see just one last time
the full hopelessness of their errand
to push her anger against his blank stare.
But I don't catch them. They're not there.

But I think of the afternoon (you told me)
you saw the back yard's maple in a storm
and whipped by winds that summer of bad weather.
You thought: *I shouldn't see this, I should be downstairs,*
but as you watched you thought the tree
was in a rage because it looked like it,
and there were no words to make it less.
Whipped by the wind on its way somewhere,
and though you knew, you said, it was a fallacy,
the tree was enraged because it stayed
right there, obedient, rooted, crazed
by simple loyalty to the ground it grew in.

Translation from an Unknown Language: The Man Who Sold His Bed

In a single village like this
where ideas run loose, our red-headed man
learned how to skip sleep: he sold his bed
and stood all night counting out stars,
beginning his sum in the west
where our mountains leap into darkness,
and ending his count in the east
where the sky falls dead into the roofs.
Every night he planted himself like a statue
in another man's yard, raising his head
before his lips began trembling with numbers.
The children called him the star hermit
and knotted his shoelaces together.
At dawn he'd sigh loudly to wake us.
When he was old and in bed, and he knew
how hard we would pay attention to him
he said there were over two thousand
thousand stars, and they talked in vibrations.
He said he'd picked up the language,
but with all of his listening, no star
would talk sense: most of them
had insane schemes about darkness
and each one thought he was God.
"The stars," he whispered, "are a mistake.
They are such unbelievable criminals."

Exasperated Political Poem

I don't care who he is or how he spells

his last name, this emperor of gunboats,
this inquisitive lobster, this full moon on vacation.
The poor might as well be crazy and drunk
and sleep at the bottom of wells,
and say their mothers' names in the streets
and weep at the sun
for all the good it will do *or has done.*
A grown man has to be crazy
to dress in rags and shout foul oaths
against the rich, right in front of their furniture,
a man has to be out of his mind
to be harmless and to pray for pneumonia.
He must be mad to lie down in a heap
like a pile of laundry, off in the corner.

I don't care what the President thinks about Jesus,

and I don't care what the pamphlets are claiming.
Soon the President will be selling the sun,
and tomorrow he will trade the moon under-the-counter.
When a sick child is eating an onion,
or two children are eating an apple,
I know they are staring off into space,
but I will not describe their skin color
or say anything about their appearance,
which is not poetry, not entertainment,
and I will not listen to the latest political

song about guns, or the morality of sugar.
Krishna, and the constellation Orion,
are speaking, and saying the usual things.
Let us rise up,
let us throw off the snow from our lips,
let us breathe in suffering and exhale charity,

let us switch this lawmaker off in midsentence
before he tries to use God against us again.

How She Knew It Was Over

She knew it was over from the corroded metal
taste of the breeze through the window
and from the silvery insects with no names—
the ones with coppery legs and small eyes
like mirrors on a garage roof—that marched,
first one and then many, out of the hole
in the white pine in the backyard,
out of it single file.

And she knew by the full-page letters
people were writing in which trenches were dug
and no one was certain which side was which
or if there was a war; she knew from
the disintegrations in trees and from accusations.
And certainly no one was kissing or cared
to make any wine, and then, oddly,
instead of saying, "Excuse me," they

were all saying, "I don't apologize,"
in a rash, low murmur. Then there was
the clarity of breakages, of broken vessels,
hunger and trash: and lectures on the necessity
of children crying quietly off by themselves.
And, as always, there were the men (and now,
finally, the women) propped up before microphones,
waving their arms, telling their terrible lies.

Machines That Make Men Happy

After dinner he worries the switch to the steep-shadowed steps
  and trudges down to the workroom

and his wife yanks the string to the attic light
  before taking the stairs in her socks

so they can both be near what they put in their hands
  with a full floor between them,

the dishes piled in the sink, the food crusting,
  the light in the living room pale,

to say, "We are home, but no, we are not here now.
  Please don't leave us a message."

The machines that make men happy are down there,
  and the nails in their jars, sung to

by an old rummage-sale radio: variable-speed grinders,
  arc welders, radial saws pressed down

with terrible force on forged metals pulled from furnaces
  and wood pincered from rivers

to be split—to be worked, bolted, to be bonded.
  It is known they have voices

and are heard all evening, the squall of drill bits
  throwing up metal and wood dust.

It's my neighbor there, chewing his unlighted cigar,
   and sometimes my own work gloves are on,

wood pressed into the clamp, the noise burning and growing
   into an intolerably beautiful cry.

When he comes up, he holds his hands out, gouged near
   the thumbnail. These are the hands

he lifts to his wife, when she is downstairs and can see him,
   a thimble still capping her finger,

and he says, "Bookshelf," or "doorframe." He can say anything.
   It's not a gift, this thing, he is giving her.

The Practice of Gentility

Despite the pumpkin placecards, and the bunny
decorations on the mantel made from
construction paper, and despite the always dying
fire and the secret-looking hors d'oeuvres,
the boy thinks, *This is serious.*

Family life puzzled Socrates—
the inverted conventions of politeness
so close to turning the soul inside out
like a harbor where the waves are stronger
than in the open sea—

and there is something mysteriously flimsy
in closeness without intimacy,
an aunt conversing about drunk
drivers and vivisection, and piles of antique
food like turkey and stuffing

sitting on the plate waiting
for something normal and legal to happen.
Lighted cigarettes in glass ashtrays,
souvenirs of a hotel in Costa Rica,
visited by the uncle who sits

with his giant-sized glass of sherry
at the piano. "Blue skies, smiling at me . . ."
This can't be why we wanted to have children,
the mother thinks, surveying the room
and trying to display a smile

she thinks of as the color of rubies.
Everyone seems to remember when the girl
was a baby, and this information
denies that she will ever achieve adult
scale. The father and mother

feel odd strains after dinner, not dessert
but the queer violence of gentility,
the ballooned self of curlicues smiling
at linen tablecloths and cut flowers.
This isn't me the unemployed cousin

says, leaning back, inhaling a Camel,
but the most polite man at the dinnertable
is the Marine, soon off for somewhere
to mine harbors where they don't do
this, exactly. He behaves, but by five

or six o'clock the party's run out
of blue sky. By now Mozart is no help
at all, and the living room sinks
bubbleless into a kind of stormy harbor.
Everyone weighs six hundred pounds,

and the chandelier wins every argument.
But charm spares a few:
the black sheep, obtuse and poverty-
stricken, sits in the ragged corner
and has no gender, and plays the music

of anger like a sidewalk musician on a winter
night roaring an aria to pigeons.
The old, too, have had enough.
They are mad and demented and always modern,
shouting against finery and silverware,

and when the front door opens, they cry,
"Don't do this, ever. Stay where you are!"

Cantata at Midnight

Wachet auf

Bach has promised that this sleep won't last:
in his cantata the voices rise
to announce the soul will levitate in time

and though the music says the music cannot be enough,
some current will pass through deadened arms,
until all the stories will be original again.

Once when I walked this scraggly forest in six inch snow
toward a long night with tiny windows and no improvement,
the nightmares drab and obvious and monochrome,

I watched a sparrow following above my head,
feathered whitebrush panhandler, blade angel wings
raising the ordinary freezing air.

Still impossible to love in dreams,
talk quietly, kiss the child, and not to see
the child explode. I'm outside anything I can imagine.

Bach claims we live through our clichés and get a life
    somewhere.
He encourages. The music is triggered out of "No,"
and never gets to "Yes," but still

and quiet as the planets seem to be,
they have been orbiting fourteen million years
and if they feel a harmony they certainly will call.

The music, tender opiate, asserts that years
from now this will all settle into place
as a chord in C# minor that everyone will hear.

The Last String Quartet of Arnold Schoenberg

In California, sick with high blood sugar,
the composer of moonlight, waltzes, and disaster

turns in his Old World body for examination
to the doctors of sun, and the doctors of air.

With his asthma Schoenberg still gasps in the oxygen
heated by tennis courts and the commerce of sea;

the upper octaves of the outdoors hamper his breathing
as does the ostinato of ocean that falls stupidly on sand.

Later, out of the hospital, Schoenberg writes to a friend
that he is working on his new string quartet

in which will appear all the complexity of his feelings
about male nurses, and I imagine him

seeing an entire human order overturned
and giving that line to the viola,

a long devious line about a young man dressed all in white
walking in, and staring pleasantly and having nothing to say,

who would fill his hours by shrugging and smiling
while flicking down a thermometer or depressing a tongue.

The eerie, beautiful American men
will effect the modulation from G major to A

as they hold his wrist lightly between their fingers and thumb
giving him fondly, this staring man, one of their familiar
   how-are-yous.

The music will be about these American children
and their evenings of honey and silk, the untorn cloth

as if there were no Laws or commandments, no Moses
to tell them *never* with a throbbing temple and a pointing finger.

This quartet won't be about the moon or the sun.
Schoenberg is done with the moon, the Earth's mad companion,

which speaks only German, and is instead at his desk writing
cadences about the way the male nurses walk silently

into the room; he is writing intervals about their delicate hands
and how at nightfall they bring him, the man from Vienna,

his food, the terrible bland chicken and juice,
how they appear in the dark to check on him,

these men of water and wind who have passed through the
   mirror
to protect and save him—these innocents, these Americans.

The One Who Didn't Drown

In the late summer sand by the dock
the grownups lean back
to let the mood of evening articulate
itself without anyone offering a comment,
while they watch the children splash and dive
and hold their shivering arms to their chests
as their skin prickles with cold water.

The amber sky dims, and moves back,
and someone has mentioned it,
but the grownups have passed on to talk
gently about a neighbor who was once alive
here in Minnesota, and the evening
almost floats like a bobber, held between
part of the day and the first few minutes of dark.

The parents laugh as if they were once
children and recognize every trick
the children try. A child notices a child is gone,
dives for him, pulls him up to the dock
where they all press their hands to his heart
and he opens his eyes and coughs, twice.

Search

One summer evening, two hours past twilight,
they are digging, the men, outside the forest's
green-blue border where the peat feels like so many sponges.

They dig for a child. The women stay home,
or, if they are here, and no one is sure if they are,
they sit on red porch chairs carried out

while they are watching the children
who run circling around the men and these women
just outside the forest. They chase fireflies

and run up to the road, to the end of nature.
Gas lanterns hissing like insects
burn down light on the men, who plop up

soil doggedly behind them. Mosquitoes swarm
in excited clouds, visible through a broken
yellowish moon that groups the men in threes:

one and one and one. A bearded man stops,
and, tipping his cap, he says,
"I'm so old I've thought of everything once.

It's nice to know I don't have to think
of anything ever again." He returns to his shovel.
What are they doing, the men, digging this hole

in the ground, or the women, watching and scolding,
pretending not to notice the men,
or the children, cartwheeling toward the highway?

I seem to see them all night,
everyone given a gender in this county
hurriedly erasing itself from the map.

IV

IMAGINARY
PAINTINGS

Diptych: Jesus and the Stone

1

The gold in *Jesus and the Stone* fell
to the painter's brush from a faithful afterlife,
homeland of dyes and tinted doors,

but where is Jesus? In the background
of this medieval altar-piece, the stone stands wide
for the gap where Christ once was but isn't

anymore, nor is he on the icy mountains
or the scared blunt sea. Jesus isn't there
and yet a crowd has gathered, foreground, all

odd proportions with knobby faces and wooden
trunks, bearded, two-dimensional figures pointing
meaning: where? where? Cobalt blue

stains the frightened market woman's dress,
and her starched white veil guards suspicions
that death is only just and finally death.

2

                                   But there, almost hidden
in the pointing crowd, right foreground,
is the returning son of man, familiar
halo like a guarantee of joyous fire

and maybe a faint smile, and maybe not
because the artist has been vague about the face
he loves; he was on his knees

and when he came to him, he fell back,
not knowing how to fill it in, that whole,
God's gold face. Two dots. A line. Astonished tears.

Madonna and Child

Her face is nothing if not perfect
as she gazes down at her brilliant child
who salutes this world
as if he knew why his face is bathed
in its gold bowl, its nimbus,
and he smiles. Something there
not tragic after all about redemption,
something inevitable and ironic,
and his mother's face is bland
with her neutral maternal
gaze, happy just to be, content
never to express. The angel
in the right-hand corner holds
his chin in his chubby hands
and floats poker-faced
in ecstasy. The mother walks
down a straight sidewalk of clouds
toward this place, down here,
where gray roofs and towers
are ringed beneath a mountain
dulled with finitude and failure,
where the faces are not so bland
as what appears in this
heavenly cloudburst of maternity
where, because the faces
are still in heaven,

they do not seek your gaze
at all and do not meet it,
expressing neither compassion
or its opposite, as blank
as trees, or stones, or bread.

Beggar in the Snow

Suppose that poverty has made him mad,
so that he sings to cows, and memorizes trees,
and wears an open mouth, and walks

barefoot like a pig in dirty snow; and suppose
his sticky yellow hair flares wildly in gusts
every time he thinks of home, of his twiceborn

mother, and suppose this beggar
with the cornsilk beard and electric teeth
has hit on every glassed-in door

and sworn to anyone he was God's handyman
in person, before the doorknobs clicked him out
into fresh air. "I was never born again,"

he says. He was a man born always,
a man who is being born right now.
In this fervent storm, the painter sees him

with an ungloved frostbite hand thrust out,
but the city has gone blind, or gone astray,
and the beggar is in a barnyard,

begging from a cow, who bears
on her patient, hammock back
a thin fabric

of thirty minutes' snow.
The beggar is singing Christmas carols to the cow.
In the distance the trees are sagging rapidly.

Death in His Kingdom

Dirty shoes and socks,
sprinkled dirt on his shirt cuff,
and unfashionable trousers: yes, Death is clothed
and sits on a chair facing away
from the human landscape behind him, these hills
experimental with figures vibrating
stiffly like cast iron flowers.

What he has isn't a face
but more a collection of features that humans have
without asking, and it's not
that he doesn't have eyes
but that they seem borrowed from sources
that no longer have any say. And it's not as if
he enjoys this portrait-sitting

or being an allegory sketched by a German
who knows him and wants him slumped
in a throne that doesn't have any shade:
no, he *doesn't* enjoy it. As usual
he's brooding at the hill's brow, the prince
of no, a geometrician with compass
and protractor, a figure whose hair is uncombed

but who loves straight lines.
At least he's not wearing a hat. Here
he's a petit-bourgeois landlord, a seedy
character with wild whitened eyes
who can fly blinded through storms
with his favorite word flung in your face
like a blood clot: *Eis eis eis*

Woman at the Riverbank

The dirty clothes heaped
on a rock behind
her, now at twilight

(pale orange haze)
she interrupts herself
and while a white

rag drips sopping
from her hand, she
half-straightens up

against her work, its
poverty, and lets
her mouth open

in surprise
to squint at a sudden
accident on the other

side. She squints
to watch a bird—
some airborne shock—

fall outside the picture
frame through the gold
bedlam

sky in front of her
(unpainted)
we do not see.

The Convalescents

In this scene the lines are not detailed

across the long green lawn where no one walks
and where the elms stand quiet in the daytime
except for a single wash of fur, a squirrel
that hurries against the coming snow.
One morning's work of brushstrokes
has brought the bugs, with tiny spectrum wings,
into the upper lefthand corner's glare.
Of course there are no sounds,
and no one here to laugh, and no sun for color:
in the distance, the working day, the mills
are sketched indifferently, and their whistles
are so distant they don't upset the sky.
The convalescents are lined up in a row.
Except for one, the painter cannot be precise
about their form. Convalescents are generic,
and there is no aesthetic precedent
for painting peacefulness that doesn't work.

This is the slowest painting in the gallery.

In the foreground is the painter's subject
around whom the air is closing in. She has
put her book aside—it's open, on the lawn,
the many pages that were once her life—
and now she gazes down, a false
madonna pose for a woman who has come this far.

She seems to pant for breath, and her face
announces to the public that she doesn't bother
much about it anymore, but, painfully,
she is also trying to smile. So the relationship
is clear: it is her son who paints
the failure of his mother's smile,
this plain expression,
the strange politeness of the dying,
as he puts her here, gray-spirited and shadowed
for this vigil, near water she cannot drink,
a woman who is all summary and conclusion.

Dr. Thomas Garvin and His Wife

An unflecked scene: clothed in blue
a young woman gazes out a curtained window,
while her husband sits self-composed across the room.
He watches nothing, this gentleman,
and no visitors give them more than half a glance:
in the gallery the mobs move past
toward the exhibit of Van Goghs,
where the crazy sunlight is lacquered gold
with heartsick energy. Back here,
the Garvins' room is dark, Victorian,
dedicated to its constructed syntax,
the empire of its gloom and shadows.
See how they sigh each quarter hour
like tired clocks, and see the hole
between them, open like an ashtray.
The way she waits there, he can't think.
She expects a glimpse of B_____,
who once stood across the street
to give a lover's sign. His open letter
is face-up on the escritoire.
The doctor, as is apparent from his lines,
has lived a decade longer than his wife
and is not her match for passion,
as is this B_____, with his top hat
and perfumed hair. See her body,
curved expectantly, with shy breasts.
His pain is prose.

Now notice how this half-lit scene
is feasting on subtractions:
the words and colors drain away, discarded.
The dim lighting sputters from two gold candles.
Here are the missing dog and cat,
here is brandy that is not set out,
here is a fire absent from the fireplace,
and over there are spines of books no one can see.
Notice? nothing visible at all.
Near the cut flowers, painfully symmetric,
is Dr. Garvin, who stares and stares
after closing *The Journal of Anatomy*
with a tired snap. Damn all this learning!
They are separated, this darkened couple,
by the space between his journal
and her dress, by all this empire furniture
muting what can be said with expensive cloth
and wood and ivory, and by the hapless marriage
that made them both into a story
their friends would tell at dinnertime
to painters, who would see it as
repressive shadowplay, a gorgeous dark.

Fleetwood Café

The sickening lunchtime sun is pale as bouillon
in the school-of-Hopper *Fleetwood Café*,

and the sky, fated to be faded blue,
is blue, but without one reason for being itself.

This hometown sky knows all your faults by heart.
A girl dressed like a clerk drinks soup and coffee

from dishes from the five-and-dime. Her hair
is starchy and hangs away. The counterman

with apron does have a face, but the sky
has robbed it of expression, like a face

(as Europeans say) that machines would build,
childish machines. No one recognizes anyone,

or gazes at the glaring light, turned on
overhead, against all sense. The special

today is Cincinnati chili, fifty cents a bowl,
and the third person, a customer, is eating it

even though his hat's still on, giving the scene
that unpleasant dollhouse feeling,

of painted ships reduced to postage stamps. Outside,
no one on the sidewalk, or sitting in the Pontiac,

or in the barbershop with its empty chairs
and pole, a hollow wooden peppermint.

Harvest Home

Dark American optimism triumphs again
when farmhands celebrate the harvest
around orange fires burning symmetrically
while the fiddlers screech the Cotton-Eyed Joe

in the background, and the kids wearing straw hats
play tag behind the dancers whose faces shine
like church altars. They are millionaires already,
it seems, and despite their scruffiness

they will know exactly how to butter their bread.
Over there, the left background, two lovers blush.
A bit of romantic comic relief.
But the paint has no doubts

in the barn's color, ready to breathe
in its hay—the barn's as red as it should be—
and no doubts in the earth, either,
pushed down by dancing, scampering feet,

but it's not Brueghel because this is America
and everyone is just kidding around. Every detail
is there for the viewer and not for the scene,
and so the viewer smiles dutifully

before passing on, forgetting the genres:
the harvest, the boy fishing, the haymow, the old
swimming hole dead as granite hung
on every wall in every small city

pleased to have illustrated happiness hanging
forgotten in the museum no one attends. A few
too many harvests in this country
and a few too many innocents filling up

Paradise and too dumb to know where they are,
these little bankers, these crazy cherubs.
In the roar and brag of American joy,
there is a baby here, mouth open, who can't cry.

River Rouge

The several rails
under cold blue

sky, and a line of car
carriers loaded in three
tiers with Fords—

white and blue and black—
and behind this Precisionist
collection of horizontals
diagonals and verticals,

the huge blue gridded tank
with FORD
printed in gigantic
cursive script
set in an oval,

and left, the beginning
of the factory itself,

and below, these things
never being quite enough,

the men, black and white,
small in comparison,
the size (here) of thumbnails

walking toward the precise
green of the factory doors
and the assembly line,

some carrying their lunch
boxes, others holding their over-
coats against the wind

unseen but which must be
there, from the papers and scrap
trash blowing across
the parking lot

Boredom of Dogs

In the surrealist *Boredom of Dogs*
    there are no dogs

    but
tin cans yawn, and
the nonessential dogs
      complain

of tedium.
The big clock says it's half-past-four.
It's always half-past-four when dogs are bored,
    when factories explode—

bang—on the horizon
    near the infant train that chugs away
to nowhere, or at least

      out of the picture. There's an artichoke
and a scoured face and long shadows drawn
on the town square. A nail's wrapped

around a piece of string. Oh, and there's
a woman who's trying to make a dash for it.
She's far away, and I wouldn't give her

half a chance, would you?
Not in this pushy
        scene, where the dogs

so often yawn,
        and the clock is striking—
            what is it?—

four-fifteen?

Rose Selavy in Oil

Academician M. Duchamp
will now commission from us her portrait in oils
of himself as Rose. Step up to the eyeholes, Moqueur,
Professor Urinal, and see this proud creation,
Mrs. C'est la Vie, dressed in a business suit
and her hair coiffed in Gothic Revival,
and Philadelphia Mint dollar bills
stuffed in her changepurse.
But look
at the medium, the oil, Rose in all that irony!

The king of the nudes wears a checkbook
of broken glass and all good fun
out on the checkerboard, near the insulted trees,

and now here's Rose sinking into your oil spill
that will sooner & later
appear on a postcard in the museum shop.
Your nude descends on an Xmas card.

I can't see her. Where is she? Oh. She's over there
by the palm trees, the soap, and the cigarettes.

Construction in black and white

---

word optics and shampoo pulled from coal.
we are here standing at the coal seam thrown across
the pennsylvania state line. make a list: that line
that line and that line, and that black and that white.
word optics. i am here, too. i have always been here.
standing behind the black of the words and the white
of the page is the "me" moving the shadows around.
when this huge abstract line is thrown over the white
and pivots like a crane to say "power"
we arrive at the black line that means coalfields
and fuel and darkness dragged up to the surface.
does this mean we are the driven and never the drivers,
does this make a magnificent asparagus and also
a fountain? i want to steal all the colors, all
the lines. i want some shadows of your own.

Black Canvas

Inside this paint is a rubber glove.

The black stain is a sidewalk running up the wall,
connecting floor to ceiling. To the interviewer,
this picture says, "No opinion." What insects
buzz in this box (30 x 38 x 1)?
Inside the paint a child blubbers softly,
pulling us into the pigment, the pitch dark

of just waking in a dark room in a fading bed
where the stranger breathes her apricot breath into the air.
If black is not a sensible emptiness
but a scent, one senses a lace curtain or a lace dress,
one smells perfume as the parents dress for dinner
in another room and call toward us where behind

this door we are supposed to be sleeping
and wait for a kiss, a peek of them sliding
in evening clothes out into the dark. Will they
be swallowed? This black reaches into the earth
and scoops out liquid nothing, attached to a hand.
It tastes the way a mouth does when it falls asleep.

Hey, bartender. Pour me some of that black.

Self-portrait as Michael Hawthorne

Behind the face, a field, it seems, of snow
and above this field an outlined clump of crisscrossed trees,
but I'm not addicted to illusion
and those might be rifles of the advancing armies
by whose mercy we might cultivate this field,
write that coda, add on this last dab of paint.
The sound behind this painting is labored breath,
the crunch of boots in snow, the muttered grumbling
of men, cursing, living in the company of men,
forwarding their heavy industry of hate.

The trees, or rifles, mean: no, not much time.
This is also what the white snow means,
it is what white paint has always meant, the high
keys on the piano played fast and quietly
as the breath grows visible in the arctic air
broken by the armies ripping down the trees
and cursing god and women; the men are coming
with guns and matches and erasers.
They carry blankness in their packs,
they love forgetting and they are any background

anywhere. It's too late in history
for his fate to have a meaning—so many faces now,
who wants to dwell on his?
The paint wants to dis-illusion the illusion of the hair
(which is thin but not on fire), the mustache,
the features—admit it—plain and ordinary
as any face, as yours, as he looks at you
through this medium. A mild man
except around the eyes, where something else is going on,
like a clock still moving in the rain,

and what matters is not what nature gave
but what's added on. What you notice is that he's outside,
he's not dressed for this, he hasn't dreamed this up,
his only plan is sickeningly modest: to make some sense
before the armies get here. It's cold. He's not complaining.
There is this moment when you think he looks you in the face
and then *we* are what is still at stake. We, and these trees,
and what the armies have left us of the earth.
All right: it's not a painting; it never was.
It was the white background, and the patterned ink.

A Chinese Poem

I am carrying a small bowl
for the wild strawberries underneath tall grass behind the house.
Early summer, and all the pheasants calling:
three short cries, mixed with the four notes of the doves.
A very thin sky and a narrow moon in it.
It's so hot the dog won't follow me,
I think he's waiting at the back door in the shade.
My shirt is near there, hanging from a branch.
Sweat flows down my face,
and I brush against the sharp points of the hawthorn.
I am singing, a little uncomfortable, but very happy . . .
These berries are ripe. There are mosquitoes here.
I fill the bowl quickly and taste one.
Bittersweet tenderness. I sniff my hand. It is so simple.
On my return the dog laps at my fingertips.

ACKNOWLEDGEMENTS

The phrase "heavy industry of hate" in "Self-portrait as Michael Hawthorne" is adapted from the poem "Gilbert & Market" by Vern Rutsala, to whom the poem is dedicated.

"Color Slides of the Warm Climate" is for Jim Krusoe.

"The Convalescents" is in memory of Mary Eaton.

About the Author

Charles Baxter is the author of the novel *First Light*, the story collections *Harmony of the World* and *Through the Safety Net*, and two earlier books of poetry. His work has appeared in *The New Yorker*, *The Paris Review*, *The Atlantic*, *Grand Street*, and many other magazines.